VERTICAL SEATTLE SERIES

LAKE UNION
THE PUBLIC FACE OF PROSPERITY

marques vickers

Lake Union: The Public Face of Prosperity
The Vertical Seattle Series: Volume One

**MARQUIS PUBLISHING
EDMONDS, WASHINGTON**

TABLE OF CONTENTS

Preface

West Lake Union
Eleven 01 Westlake Building
AGC Building
The Lake Union Building
1633 Westlake Avenue North
PEMCO Building

About the Author

Version 1.1

Published by Marquis Publishing
Part of Marquis Enterprises
Edmonds, Washington USA

Vickers, Marques, 1957

LAKE UNION: The Public Face of Prosperity
Vertical Seattle Series, Volume One

To My Daughters Charline and Caroline.

The Public Face of Prosperity
The heightening of the downtown Seattle skyline mirrors the prosperity and expansion of the business core. This change in complexion is most evident along the shoreline of Lake Union, a freshwater passage contained entirely within Seattle's city limits.

Lake Union was originally formed by the melting of the Vashon Glacier waters and officially named by Seattle pioneer Thomas Mercer in 1854. Mercer correctly forecasted that with effective damming and canals, the eventual union of Lake Washington and Puget Sound could be completed. The Duwamish and Chinook native tribes called the body small waters.

The Boeing Corporation initiated production facilities in 1916. The shoreline for decades remained principally shipyards, wharfs, sawmills and diminutive restaurant and retail outlets. The high technology industry and particularly Amazon.com has completely altered the commercials emphasis. The chronic Seattle housing shortage has accentuated a similar boom for elevated residential properties.

Staggering glass monoliths have continued to proliferate amongst the welcoming neighborhoods of South Lake Union and periphery sections on the eastern and western shores. Proponents of contemporary progress have welcomed the expansion of mixed-use commercial office, retail, hotel accommodations and permanent living spaces. Assuming that the ambitious pace continues, South Lake Union will consolidate its gateway status towards the historic downtown core. In the process, the construction is eliminating generations of low-rise buildings and structural eyesores of modest or no local architectural significance.

The rapid progression has prompted criticism based on the accompanying traffic congestion, skyrocketing leases and parking scarcity. Light rail programs may alleviate some of these concerns. Many critics have cited that the city of Seattle was never intended nor proactively planned to become a major urban center. The infrastructure to accommodate its growth is being installed on a catch-up basis.

The argument may be valid, but the city planners of Seattle appear fully committed towards growth and elevated expansion. Activist demands for restraint and moderation are generally muffled amidst the momentum of increasing space demands, public hearings, zoning variances, demolition and construction. The nature of aggressive growth does not historically pause.

The Lake Union shoreline has become forever changed. Most of the completed high-rise buildings featured in this edition are less than ten years old. Numerous more are anticipated and currently in diverse stages of planning and completion. This edition is intended to document the changes in the present tense. Clearly, however, downtown Seattle's future is oriented towards an increasing vertical expansion.

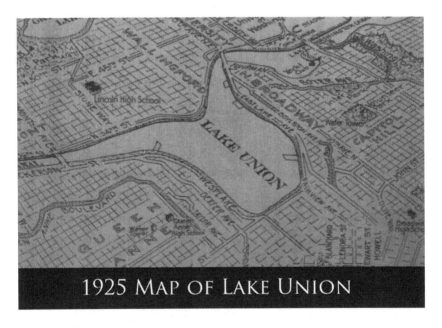

1925 MAP OF LAKE UNION

SOUTH LAKE UNION

Pontius Building
Commercial Office Complex
425 Pontius Avenue North
4-Stories, Completed: 1982

Vue Research Center
500-530 Fairview Avenue North
7-Stories, Completed: 2016
Major Tenants: Novo Nordisk and Nano String

Urban Union Office Complex
(Ownership: Amazon.com)
501 Fairview Avenue North
12-Stories, Under Construction, Completion Date 2017

400 Fairview Avenue North
13-Stories, Completed: 2015
Major Tenants: Tommy Bahama, Car Toys/ Wireless Advocates,
Impinj Incorporated and Stantec

425 Fairview Avenue North
405-433 Fairview Avenue North
24-Story Tower and 7-Story Mid-Rise
Mixed Use Retail and Residential
Under Construction, Estimated Completion Date 2018

Amazon.com Fiona Building
500-530 Boren Avenue North
5-Stories, Completed: 2009
Additional Tenant:
Swedish South Lake Union Primary Care

Amazon.com Obidos Building
551 Boren Avenue North
5-Stories, Completed: 2010

Troy Block Complex
(Ownership: Amazon.com)
300 Boren Avenue North
13-Stories, First Building Completed: 2016, Second Building
Under Construction with Expected Completion Date 2017

Amazon.com Dawson Building
345 Boren Avenue North
11-Stories, Completed: 2011

Amazon.com Ruby Building
333 Boren Avenue North
5-Stories, Completed: 2011

Amazon.com Wainwright Building
535 Terry Avenue North
5-Stories, Completed: 2010
Named after the first Amazon book client John Wainwright

46

48

Amazon.com Rufus Building
550 Terry Avenue North
5-Stories, Completed: 2010

Moxy Hotel (Marriott Property)
1016 Republican
8-Stories, 146 Rooms, Under Construction, Completion 2017

Amazon.com Day North Building (Headquarters)
440 Terry Avenue North
6-Stories, Completed: 2009

Amazon.com Day South Building (Headquarters)
410 Terry Avenue North
5-Stories, Completed: 2010

Institute for Systems Biology Building
Northeastern University Seattle
401 Terry Avenue North
4-Stories, Completed: 2004

Group Health Building
321 Terry Avenue North
4-Stories, Completed: 2007

The Allen Institute for Brain Science
615 Westlake Avenue North
6-Stories, Completed: 2015

Amazon Bigfoot Building
515 Westlake Avenue North
6-Stories, Completed: 2014

428 Westlake Avenue North Building
6-Stories, Completed: 2004

Westlake Terry Building
320 Westlake Avenue North
6-Stories, Completed: 2007
Tenants: Microsoft and Gary Manuel Studio

Seattle BioMed Building
307 Westlake Avenue North
5-Stories, Completed: 2003
Tenants: Juno Therapeutics, Seattle BioMed and Center For
Infectious Diseases

University of Washington Medicine Research Complex
Institute of Translational Health Sciences
850 Republican Street (Covers the entire block area between
Republican and Mercer Streets and Eighth and Ninth Avenue)
Five Buildings including the Rosen and Brotman Research
Buildings and Administration Building
Opened 1982

Amazon.com Nessie Building
500 Ninth Avenue North
5-Stories, Completed: 2014

Amazon.com Brazil Building
400 Ninth Avenue North
12-Stories, Completed: 2015

Amazon Apollo Building
325 Ninth Avenue North
12-Stories, Completed: 2015

The Alexandria Center
400 Dexter Avenue North
12-Stories, Under Construction, Completion Date 2017
Future Home of Juno Therapeutics

EAST LAKE UNION

Fred Hutchinson Cancer Research Center
Complex of Thirteen Buildings 1100 Fairview Avenue North,
1100 Eastlake Avenue North and
823 Yale Avenue
Opened: 1993

Zymogenetics Building
1201 Eastlake Avenue North
7-Stories, Completed: 1914 (Renovated 1994)

WEST LAKE UNION

Eleven 01 Westlake Building
1101 Westlake Avenue North
6-Stories, Completed: 2016

AGC Building
1200 Westlake Avenue North
11-Stories, Completed: 1971

1505 Westlake Avenue North
10-Stories, Completed: 1994
Tenants: SRM Reproductive Medicine Seattle, Dassault Systems,
Crown Castle and Psychiatric Medicine Associates

The Lake Union Building
1700 Westlake Avenue North
7-Stories, Completed: 1970

1633 Westlake Avenue North
4-Stories, Completed: 1971

PEMCO Building
1300 Dexter Avenue North
5-Stories, Completed: 1983

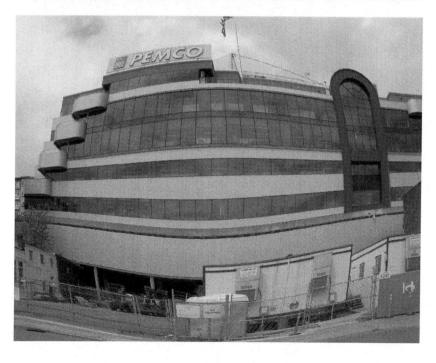

Visual Artist, Writer and Photographer Marques Vickers is a California native presently living in the San Francisco Bay Area and Seattle, Washington regions.

He was born in 1957 and raised in Vallejo, California. He is a 1979 Business Administration graduate from Azusa Pacific University in the Los Angeles area. Following graduation, he became the Public Relations and ultimately Executive Director of the Burbank Chamber of Commerce between 1979-84. He subsequently became the Vice President of Sales for AsTRA Tours and Travel in Westwood between 1984-86.

Following a one-year residence in Dijon, France where he studied at the University of Bourgogne, he began Marquis Enterprises in 1987. His company operations have included sports apparel exporting, travel and tour operations, wine brokering, publishing, rare book and collectibles reselling. He has established numerous e-commerce, barter exchange and art websites including MarquesV.com, ArtsInAmerica.com, InsiderSeriesBooks.com, DiscountVintages.com and WineScalper.com.

Between 2005-2009, he relocated to the Languedoc region of southern France. He concentrated on his painting and sculptural work while restoring two 19th century stone village residences. His figurative painting, photography and sculptural works have been sold and exhibited internationally since 1986. He re-established his Pacific Coast residence in 2009 and has focused his creative productivity on writing and photography.

His published works span a diverse variety of subjects including true crime, international travel, California wines, architecture, history, Southern France, Pacific Coast attractions, auctions, fine art marketing, poetry, fiction and photojournalism.

He has two daughters, Charline and Caroline who presently reside in Europe.

BOOKS:
Marketing and Buying Fine Art Online, Allworth Press, New York NY (2005)
Making Auction Pay, Marquis Publications, Vallejo CA. (2014)
Unicorns and Dark Chocolate: Eros, Aphrodesia and Existence, Marquis Publications, Vallejo CA (2014)
Amour, Wine and Real Estate, Marquis Publications, Vallejo CA (2014)
Flamenco Jondo: The Paintings of Marques Vickers, Marquis Publications, Vallejo CA (2014)
The Ultimate Guide to Selling Art Online, Marquis Publications, Vallejo CA (2014)
The Lafayette White Cross Memorial, Marquis Publications, Vallejo CA (2014)
2014 Napa Valley Earthquake, Marquis Publications, Vallejo CA (2014)
Fish Head Beach: The Silent and Senseless Murders of Lindsay Cutshall and Jason Allen, Marquis Publications, Vallejo CA (2014)

Muse One: Pantera Linda, Marquis Publications, Vallejo CA (2014)
Nature As Art: One, Marquis Publications, Vallejo CA (2014)
Springtime in New England, Marquis Publications, Vallejo CA (2014)
San Antonio Riverwalk, Marquis Publications, Vallejo CA (2014)
Ruined Castles and Phantom Memories, Marquis Publications, Vallejo CA (2014)
Sand and Water: Desert and Seascapes, Marquis Publications, Vallejo CA (2014)
Napa Rebuilds: Two Months Following Their Devastating Earthquake, Marquis Publications, Vallejo CA (2014)
The 2014 Napa Valley Wine Harvest, Marquis Publications, Vallejo CA (2014)
The Topography of Evil: Notorious Northern California Murder Sites, Marquis Publications, Vallejo CA (2015)
The Disappearing Women, Marquis Publications, Morro Beach CA (2015)
Five Month of Renovation After the 2014 Napa Earthquake, Marquis Publications, Morro Bay CA (2015)
100 Famous Phobias and Obsessions: An Entertaining Portrayal of Anxiety, Fears and Insecurity As Artwork, Marquis Publications, Morro Bay CA (2015)
Visions of Neo-Urbania: The Reinvention of Contemporary Metropolitan Vertical Living and Commerce, Marquis Publications, Tacoma WA (2015)
Nature As Art Two: Photography and Abstract Paintings of Marques Vickers, Marquis Publications, Tacoma WA (2015)
Morro Rock: Veiled Bridge of the Nine Sisters, Marquis Publications, Tacoma WA (2015)
Eternal Spring Street: Los Angeles' Architectural Reincarnation, Marquis Publications, Tacoma WA (2015)
The Reflective Powers of Water As Visual Alchemy, Marquis Publications, Tacoma WA (2015)

*Jimi Hendrix, Bruce and Brandon Lee and the Lakeview
Cemetery Seattle: Entombing Our Icons*, Marquis Publications,
Renton WA (2015)
The Artistic Properties of Reflective Glass, Marquis Publications,
Renton WA (2015)
The Glass Curtain Architecture of Bellevue, Washington,
Marquis Publications, Renton WA (2015)
Murder in California: Notorious California Murder Sites,
Marquis Publications, Renton WA (2015)
*Coffee Anarchists of the World Unite: The Italian Roasted Elixirs
of Tacoma, Washington*, Marquis Publications, Renton WA
(2015)
*The Abandoned Western Cascade Mountain Railroad Tunnels
and 1910 Wellington Avalanche*, Marquis Publications, Renton
WA (2015)
*The 2014 Napa Earthquake and Anniversary Aftermath: A
Fourteenth Month Retrospective Into Historical Downtown
Napa*, Marquis Publications, Concord CA (2015)
Murder in Washington: The Topography of Evil, Marquis
Publications, Larkspur CA (2016)
*The Architectural Elevation of Technology: A Photo Survey of 75
Silicon Valley Headquarters*, Marquis Publishing, Edmonds, WA
(2016)
*Reinventing Broadway Street: Los Angeles Architectural
Reincarnation*, Marquis Publishing, Edmonds, WA (2016)
*So You Think You Know California Wine? (2016) The Grape
Divide: Demystifying the Economics of Wine*, Marquis
Publishing, Edmonds, WA (2016)
Unseen Marin: The Waterways of Marin County, California,
Marquis Publications, Edmonds, WA (2016)
Tulip Universe, Marquis Publications, Edmonds, WA (2016)
Unseen Marin: The Waterways of Mill Valley, Marquis
Publications, Edmonds, WA (2016)
Unseen Marin: The Waterways of Central Marin County,
Marquis Publications, Edmonds, WA (2016)

Unseen Marin: The Waterways of San Rafael and Fairfax,
Marquis Publications, Edmonds, WA (2016)
*When Letters Still Mattered: An Autobiography Based on
Correspondence*, Marquis Publications, Edmonds, WA (2016)

Made in the USA
San Bernardino, CA
23 January 2017